GUAC
-A-
MOLE

An Avocado Smashing Game

T0364030

RP Minis®
Hachette Book Group
1290 Avenue of the Americas, New York, NY 10104
www.runningpress.com
@Running_Press

First Edition: September 2024

Published by RP Minis, an imprint of Hachette Book Group, Inc.
The RP Minis name and logo is a registered trademark of Hachette
Book Group, Inc.

Running Press books may be purchased in bulk for business, educational,
or promotional use. For more information, please contact your local
bookseller or the Hachette Book Group Special Markets Department at
Special.Markets@hbgusa.com.

The publisher is not responsible for websites (or their content) that are
not owned by the publisher.

Design by Jason Kayser

ISBN: 978-0-7624-8715-8

Contents

~~

Introduction

~~~

If you've ever enjoyed whacking a pretend mole on the head at your local arcade, then Guac-a-Mole is the game for you! Inspired by the popular Whac-a-Mole game, Guac-a-Mole gives you the opportunity to bop an avocado-mole (aka a guac-a-mole!), with a mini mashing tool. The object of the game is to whack as many as you can

when they light up, before time runs out.
You can play the game on your desk or on
the go, but whichever way you play it, be
quick . . . They may be small, but these
feisty guac-a-moles will disappear faster
than you can say "guacamole!!"

History of
Whacking Games

〜

The original whacking game was invented
in 1975 by Kazuo Yamada. The aim of
the game was to whack as many moles
as you could with a mallet before they
disappeared back into the "soil." The con-
cept proved so successful in Japan that it
soon went worldwide, with the first US
version arriving in late 1976. After some

modifications, the famous Whac-a-Mole game was born, and in the 1980s it became one of the most well-liked games to be found in arcades and fairgrounds.

Since then, whacking games have remained popular with children and adults of all ages. So much so that you can now bop the likes of frogs, space creatures, crocodiles, dinosaurs, and vegetables, not only in arcades but also in your home and on your console.

Hints and Tips to Win at Guac-a-Mole

To get as many points as you can, it's important to have a keen eye and a flexible wrist! You can warm your wrist up first, with a few rotations clockwise and counterclockwise. When playing, always keep your eyes on the board, and your mind on the game, ready for the guac-a-moles to light up.

Other Ways to Play

~

While Guac-a-Mole is great when played as intended, you can make up your own rules, too. For instance, why not try to use your left hand if right-handed, or your right hand if left-handed? You could also try just hitting particular guac-a-moles, such as the center mole, or those on the left or right. Resisting the urge to whack every guac-a-mole that pops up is much harder than you might think! If there is more than one player, why not play against each other, or even in teams? The highest combined score of each team is the winner.

Avocados: A Favorite Fruit

Avocados are an extremely popular fruit, and the wonderful inspiration for our "mashed up" game of Guac-a-Mole. They are a great choice for breakfast, lunch, or whenever you're feeling a little hungry! They come in many shapes and have a large pit in the middle. When the fruit is ripe and ready to eat, the green flesh will have a buttery texture. If your avocado can stand a little pressure from your fingertips, then it is ready to be eaten. How can you tell if it is overly ripe? Well, if your finger presses easily and deeply into the avocado, chances are that it has gone past its best, and will not taste good.

Because avocados need a mixture of sunshine, rain, and a cooler evening atmosphere, they are generally grown in hotter countries. They originated in Mexico, and at least half of the world's avocado supply still comes from there,

but they can also be found in Peru and Kenya. The fruit was introduced to the United States in the 1800s, and California now produces the majority of the USA's supply.

There are various types of avocados, including Hass, Mendez, and Criollo. They are rich in nutrients and a good source of fiber, vitamin C and E, folate, potassium, monosaturated fat, and minerals such as iron, copper, and potassium. It is said that the fruit can lower cholesterol and is good for heart health.

How Avocados Can Be Used

The most popular way to use avocados is as a food, or an accompaniment to various dishes. Guacamole originates from Mexico, and is made from ripe avocados, smashed with salt and sometimes a little lime or lemon juice, but did you know that you can also add tomatoes, corn, or even fruit to the mixture? However you wish to eat it, you should always prepare guacamole (and any other avocado dish) shortly before you intend to serve it, because avocados have a tendency to go brown after cutting.

While guacamole is the most famous of all avocado dishes, fans of the versatile fruit have also been known to use it as an accompaniment to pasta or rice, in salsa, smashed on toast (with a little olive oil, salt, and pepper), in a wrap or on a salad, grilled, in soup, pickled, grated into cooked scrambled eggs, sliced onto pizza or a burger, or

pureed as an alternative to butter or mayonnaise. Halved avocados (minus the pit!) can also be stuffed with your favorite food, such as eggs, bacon, fish, chicken, or fruit. In the 1920s, it was fashionable to rub the flesh into a pulp, add lemon juice, olive oil, and seasoning, and then serve it in the avocado shell/skin.

Avocados are mainly associated with savory dishes, but did you know that they can also be added to sweet recipes, such as smoothies, chocolate mousse, jellies, cakes, pancakes, and even ice cream?

Skincare and Avocados

~~~

In 1856, it was reported that an avocado tree in the West Indies produced a fruit so high in oil that it could be used as a skin illuminator and in the manufacture of soap. Then in the 1930s, beauty company Coty boasted that their new Beauty Milk was a fantastic, pore-deep cleanser, thanks to the main ingredient—avocado oil. Their

Avocado Beauty Soap declared that "You will quickly appreciate its soothing effect upon the skin, it's high curative quality and rich soft lather." Customers were encouraged to use it regularly for a perfect complexion. So popular were the women's products, that the brand soon added shaving cream for men, too.

Since then, avocado has been a favorite ingredient in many different beauty products, such as shampoo, conditioner, moisturizer, primer, and beard balm, thanks to its ability to hydrate and moisturize. It is also claimed to improve skin texture and health, as well as reduce inflammation.

Some people make their own face mask by pureeing avocado with honey and vinegar and applying the mixture to the face (avoiding eyes of course!). After it has dried, it is washed off and moisturizer is applied as needed.

Avocados in Popular Culture

It doesn't matter where you go, avocado-themed products and gift items seem to be everywhere. A quick trip to the store will conjure up avocado on apparel, games (such as this one!), cuddly toys, blankets, and so much more. Our favorite fruit has also been featured in various songs, such as "The Avocado Song" by Alton Eugene,

"Guacamole" by GoNoodle, and "Avocado Dance" by Sefi Zisling, as well as being used as characters in cartoons and books.

Did You Know?

- The term Whac-a-Mole doesn't just apply to a game. It is also used when a series of problems keep popping up, and a solution for each one needs to be found. The term is used frequently by police and the military.

- In the 1920s, avocados were nick-
  named, "Alligator pears," because it
  was thought that if anyone took a
  bite out of one (skin and all), they'd be
  repulsed and throw it to the alligators!
  Then at the start of the twentieth cen-
  tury, the fruit was often known as
  vegetable marrows, because of their
  marrow-like taste, or midshipman's
  butter, because of its buttery taste.
  By the time the 1920s came around, it
  was believed that only the poshest of
  people would ever eat avocados!

- Celebrities who are said to be fans
  of avocados include actresses
  Jennifer Aniston and Kristen Bell,
  racing driver Lewis Hamilton, and
  actor Chris Hemsworth. Singer Miley
  Cyrus, meanwhile, is such a fan that
  she even has an avocado tattoo!